Molecule:
pages 18, 19, 22, 23

Ion:
pages 18, 19, 20, 21

Nerve cells:
pages 16, 17, 18,
19, 26, 27, 28, 29

Impulses:
pages 16, 17, 24, 25,
26, 27, 40, 41

Sight: pages 24, 25

Dendrite: pages 16, 17

Perception:
pages 40, 41

Animal brains:
pages 2, 3, 14, 15

Neurotransmitters: pages 22, 23

Sleep:
pages 42, 43

Synapse:
pages 16, 17, 18, 19,
20, 21, 22, 23, 26,
27, 28, 29

Axon:
pages 16, 17, 18, 19

DEC   2010

BRAIN

A 21st Century look
at a 400-million-year-old organ

by Rob DeSalle and Patricia J. Wynne

with Wallace and Darwin,
the museum mice

Based on an
exhibition at the
American Museum
of Natural
History

Bunker Hill Publishing

Hi, we're Wallace and Darwin! We're museum mice. We like science, so we live in an enormous natural history museum.
I'm Darwin. This museum has dinosaurs, sharks, lions, tigers, prehistoric humans, insects — just about everything!
And I'm Wallace. There are labs for genetics and tons of cabinets full of specimens. And lots of examples from cultures around the world!
There's so much stuff here that Wallace and I have lots to be curious about. For instance, did you ever wonder why all the animals in this museum do the things they do?
I think, therefore I am. It must be our brains!
Right! It's the brain that does it all. That's why now we are going to take a journey into the brain!

Hmmmm . . .
What are all of
these numbers?

That's the weight of
each animal's brain.

So, a beaver's
brain weighs 45 grams
and a squirrel's brain is
only 7.6 grams!

And the
way brains
evolved in
these animals
is awesome.

Some animals must
have really small brains —
like cats. I hate cats.

As we'll see,
size doesn't
matter when it
comes to the
brain.

Brain weight in grams . . . .

3

ONE GRAM

1,300 GRAMS

What's all the hoopla about a brain, Wallace? It's just three pounds in humans, and a whole gram in us mice. How hard can it be to figure out a brain?

I've heard most people think a brain works like a computer.

Messy Brains

Nearly all animals have brains or some kind of nervous system. As brains evolved, they did not evolve perfectly. When a computer is built, engineers take advantage of mistakes and experiences they have seen in earlier computers. The design of computers can improve, based on these experiences. When brains change, they follow the rules of evolution. One rule is that evolution cannot produce new things in organisms that are too terribly different from the ancestor of the organism. Another rule is that not all evolutionary changes make sense, and can appear to be random events. This happens a lot in small populations. These rules ensure that the brain in organisms is pretty much what neuroscientist Gary Marcus calls a KLUGE. Kluges are contraptions that look like junk and don't work as efficiently as they should, but nevertheless **do** work.

I heard that too, but many scientists don't think our brains are like computers at all.

Don't our brains do math, make decisions, and have memory like computers?

CONTRAPTION ZONE
Computers are built very logically, so there is little waste in the programs and hardware of a computer. I don't think animal brains are put together that logically.
So maybe animal brains are more like contraptions.
Maybe they are a little like Rube Goldberg machines. You know, those crazy machines with all kinds of moving parts made from junk?
Alright!

Since the brain is so important, lots of scientists study it.

And because the brain is so complicated, there are many different subjects to study.

HUMAN BRAIN

Hey, Wallace! Scientists could study the **shape** of brains. Brain shape *must* be different between us and cats!

CAT BRAIN

MOUSE BRAIN

Looks like it! And scientists study the **chemicals** that make brains work. What else do scientists study about brains?

CHEMICAL MESSENGERS

What kinds of scientists study brains?

There are many kinds of scientists who study brains and the mind. Neuroscientists study the functioning of the brain. Neuroanatomists study the shape and parts of the brain. They use all sorts of technology to look at brains and to study the parts of the brain that are involved in aspects of the mind. Neurophysiologists study the chemistry of the brain. Neuropathologists study brain diseases. And Neurolinguists study how the brain produces and controls language. There is one scientist who studies brains who doesn't have a "neuro" in front of her specialty. These scientists are the Psychologists who study the behavior of people. Psychologists help us understand how the human brain and mind work. Neurobiology is one of the most exciting areas of science, because it combines many new approaches and technology to understand the brain.

DNA

And there are scientists who study the *genes* that are important for the working brain. That's my favorite.

Don't forget the scientists who study how the brain affects the way animals behave. They try to make links between the brain and what they call the *mind*.

Do you notice, Wallace, that there aren't many plants displayed in our museum?
Yep. This museum is devoted almost entirely to animals. Maybe it's because they have brains. I wonder if plants have brains?
EAST AFRICAN ELEPHANT

Nope. They don't have brains, but they do have some of the same genes and chemicals that are used in animal brains.

Is that why you call me a pea-brain sometimes?

PEA PLANT

Do Plants have brains?

To be successful, all cells need to communicate. Even tiny bacterial cells need to communicate with one another. To do this, chemicals made by one bacterium stick to the cell surface of another. This causes a reaction in the second bacterium that makes the cell respond in some way. Plants and very simple animals without brains also have cells in their bodies that communicate with each other. It is as if cells are talking to each other using chemicals. Some plants have a gene that makes a protein that actually acts like a nervous system protein. In fact, this protein is very similar in shape and size to animal proteins in nerve cells. Does this mean plants think? Most definitely not! It does mean that plant cells can communicate with each other using the same genes and same chemical reactions that animals do.

No! That wouldn't be nice. But it does mean that plants are related to animals through their genes.

PLANT CELLS COMMUNICATING

Gosh, Darwin for someone with a whole gram brain, you ask a lot of questions.

MOON JELLYFISH

I was wondering if really squishy things have brains? For instance, do sponges have brains? What about jellyfish?

SPONGES

Do really squishy things have brains?

Lower animals like sponges have many of the same genes used in higher animal nervous systems. They can make the proteins that work in the nervous system, but sadly for sponges their genes don't make brains. Jellyfish, part of a group of animals called Cnidaria, have neural nets throughout their bodies. These neural nets are the cnidarian nervous system. Some scientists think that the neural nets aren't the same kind of nervous system or even made up of the same kind of nerve cells as in more complex animals. This would mean that nerve cells evolved twice in the history of animals on earth: once in the simple animals like cnidaria, and once in the more complex animals, like ourselves.

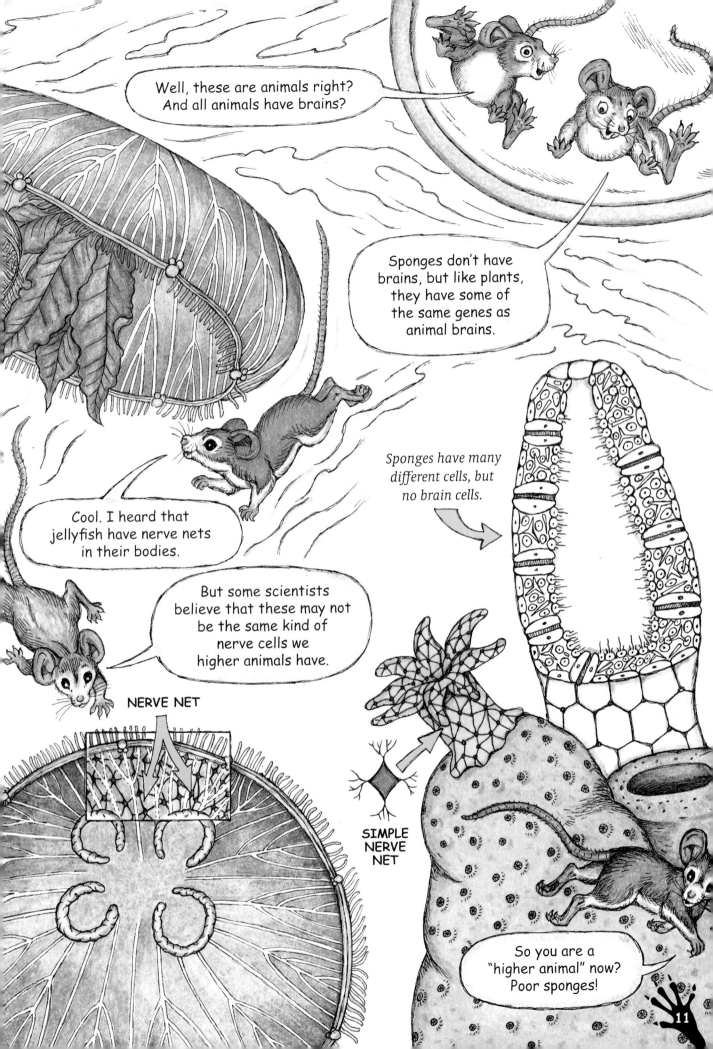

I bet fly brains are pretty small.

Yep, you would win that bet. But just because they are small, doesn't mean they don't work.

Do really tiny animals like flies and worms have brains?

It is a good bet that the nerve cells of higher animals like flies, worms, and ourselves are the same kind of cells. The same chemicals and genes are involved in the function of the brain and the working of the nervous systems in all higher animals. But the kinds of brains in higher animals are very different. A fly brain is made up of about ten thousand cells. (Compare that to the human brain which has about 50–100 billion cells). Worms like the nematode *Caenorhabditis elegans* only have about 1,000

BRAIN

NERVOUS SYSTEM

LEECH NERVES

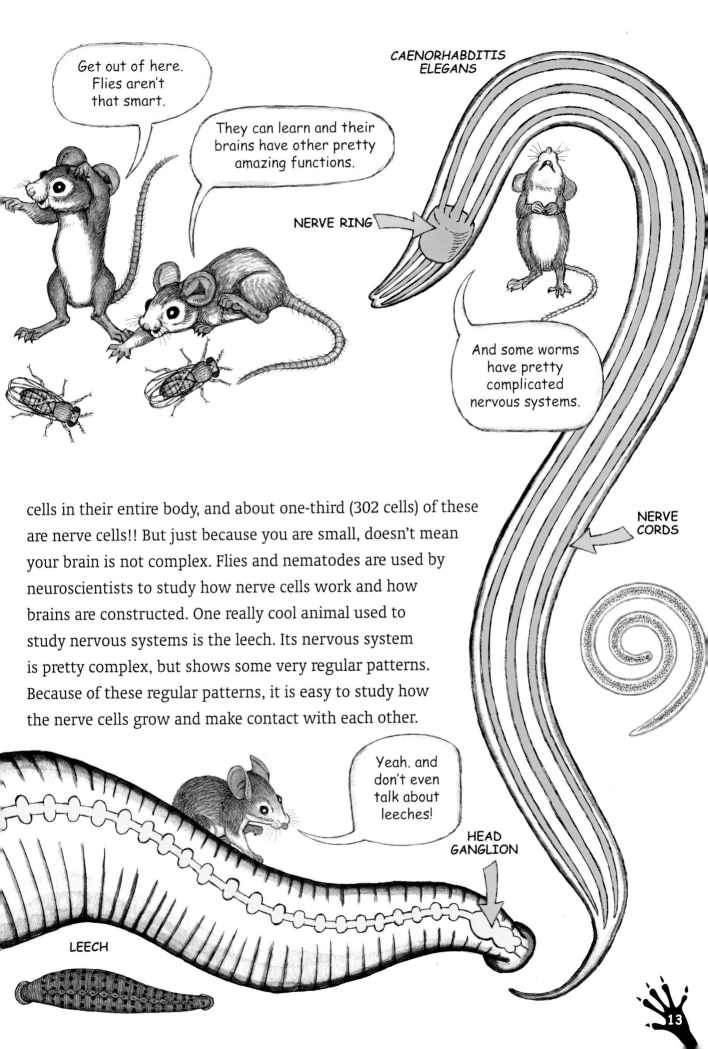

Get out of here. Flies aren't that smart.

They can learn and their brains have other pretty amazing functions.

CAENORHABDITIS ELEGANS

NERVE RING

And some worms have pretty complicated nervous systems.

NERVE CORDS

cells in their entire body, and about one-third (302 cells) of these are nerve cells!! But just because you are small, doesn't mean your brain is not complex. Flies and nematodes are used by neuroscientists to study how nerve cells work and how brains are constructed. One really cool animal used to study nervous systems is the leech. Its nervous system is pretty complex, but shows some very regular patterns. Because of these regular patterns, it is easy to study how the nerve cells grow and make contact with each other.

Yeah. and don't even talk about leeches!

HEAD GANGLION

LEECH

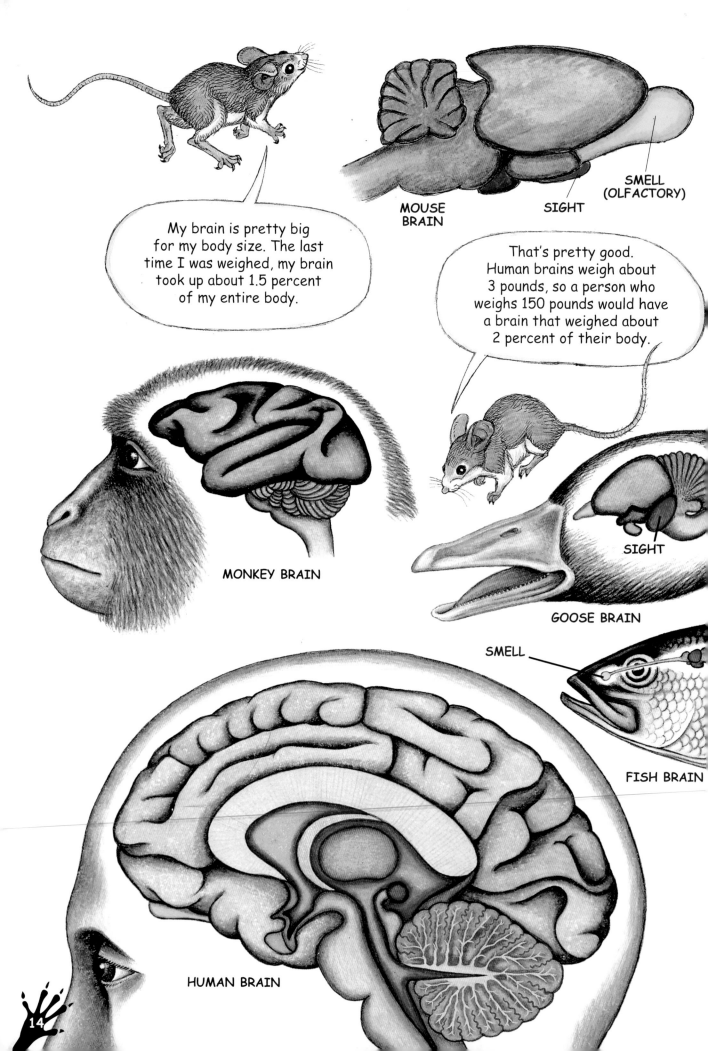

MOUSE
BRAIN

SIGHT

SMELL
(OLFACTORY)

My brain is pretty big for my body size. The last time I was weighed, my brain took up about 1.5 percent of my entire body.

That's pretty good. Human brains weigh about 3 pounds, so a person who weighs 150 pounds would have a brain that weighed about 2 percent of their body.

MONKEY BRAIN

SIGHT

GOOSE BRAIN

SMELL

FISH BRAIN

HUMAN BRAIN

A blue whale has the largest brain on the planet, yet it's brain only takes up about 0.01 percent of its body.

WHALE BRAIN

So that means we are 100 times smarter than whales?

CANARY BRAIN

Does the size of the brain in an organism matter?

Some people think that the size of the brain determines how smart an animal is. This is hard to prove or disprove, because what we humans define as "smart" might be entirely different to a mouse. For instance, while the human and mouse brains look similar at first glance, when we look closer, parts of the brain are different sizes. The mouse brain has a huge bulb at the front called the olfactory (smell) bulb. The same bulb in humans is quite small. This is because mice use smell as a major means of sensing the outside world. Another cool comparison is the brains of birds that sing and the brains of birds that don't. Singing birds have much more complex auditory systems in their brains than birds without song.

Probably not. But our brains take up 100 times more space in our bodies than whale brains do in theirs.

SNAKE BRAIN

CAT BRAIN

SMELL

OPPOSSUM BRAIN

FROG BRAIN

Nerve Cells! Getting down to business.

Human brains are made of nerve cells called neurons, about 100,000,000,000 of them. That is a lot of cells, but what makes the brain so complex is that these cells connect to each other through synapses. There are 1,000 to 10,000 connections made from each nerve cell. Most neurons are small, but a neuron in the giraffe that goes from toe to neck is 15 feet long!

The body of the neuron contains the nucleus where all the DNA of the cell is stored. Projections called dendrites come out of the cell body. Sometimes long projections sprout from the neuron reaching to other nerve cells. These long projections are called axons. Axons are covered by a protein called myelin. This myelin sheath protects the axon. At the tips of each axon, synapses form with other nerve cells. Synapses are really just a space between the axon and another nerve cell where chemicals and molecules can be transferred. The interchange of these chemicals and molecules is what makes your nervous system work.

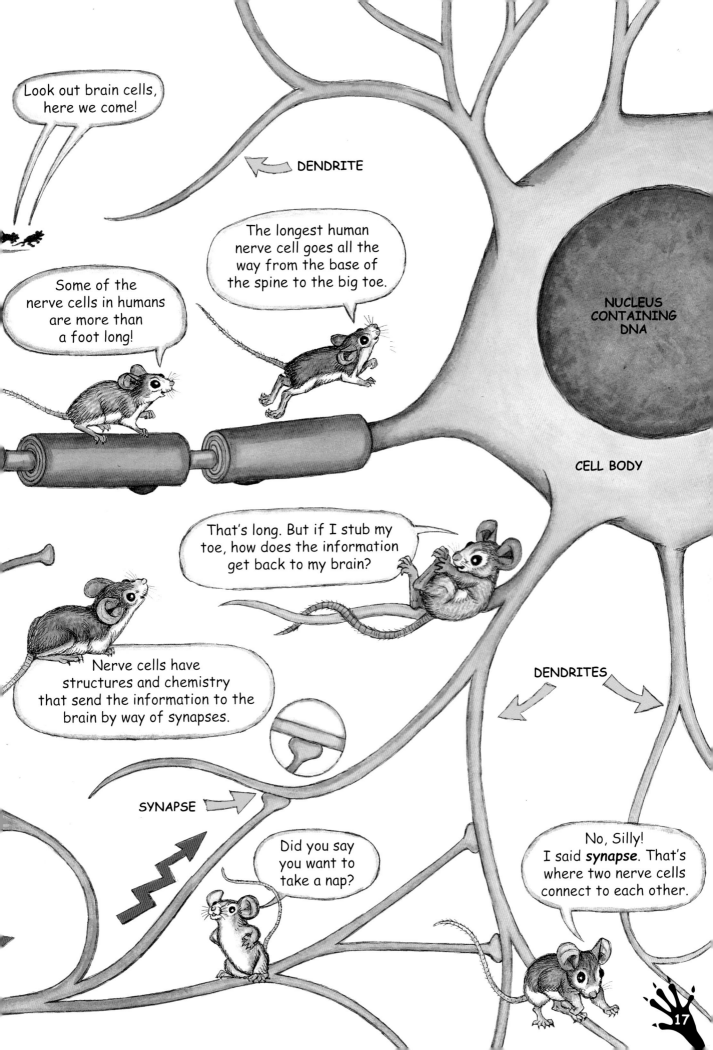

What happens at the chemical level when my brain works?

Neurons send impulses from one cell to another electrochemically. Where does the electricity come from? From ions that change their concentrations from one side of the synapse to the other. This changes the electrical potential across the synapse. Ions have charges because they are made up of atoms that have electrons. Atoms can then change their electrical states by losing or gaining electrons. That changes the electrical charge of the ion. The important chemicals that change charges at the synapse are potassium, sodium, calcium, and chloride atoms.

NERVE CELL

ELECTRICAL IMPULSE

So Darwin, we know our nervous systems work by sending out electrical currents.

Absolutely! That's where the chemicals and molecules at the synapse start working.

The giant axon of the squid is being moved by needles. See the fingertip of the scientist!

But do you know which animal they studied to get this picture of how nerve cells work?

Sure do! A squid! Squids have a huge nerve that runs from their brains all the way to their tails. It tells their tails to wag.

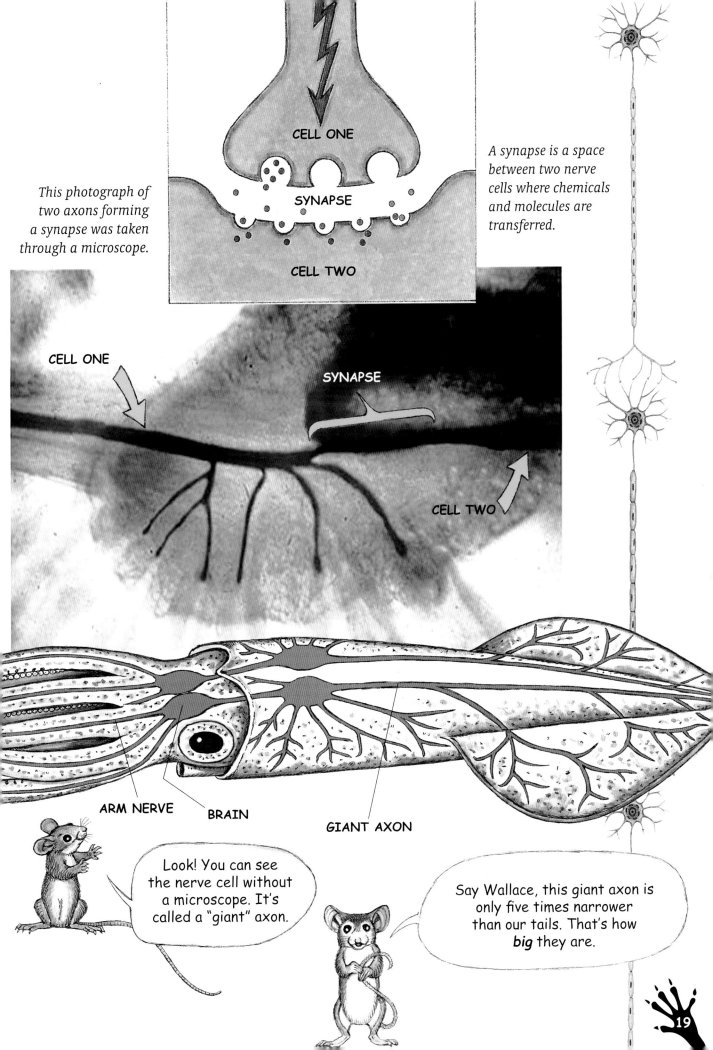

This photograph of two axons forming a synapse was taken through a microscope.

CELL ONE

SYNAPSE

CELL TWO

A synapse is a space between two nerve cells where chemicals and molecules are transferred.

CELL ONE

SYNAPSE

CELL TWO

ARM NERVE   BRAIN

GIANT AXON

Look! You can see the nerve cell without a microscope. It's called a "giant" axon.

Say Wallace, this giant axon is only five times narrower than our tails. That's how *big* they are.

Changing potential across the synapse

Neurons that aren't sending messages to other cells across synapses are said to be "at rest." But this term is a little misleading, because there is always an electrical charge across the synapse (about 70 millielectron volts). The difference in charge is caused by the difference in the concentration of potassium, chloride, magnesium, and sodium ions in the two cells. When impulses caused by these ions run down the axon to the synapse, neurophysiologists say that the synapse is ready to fire, spike, or pulse. When a synapse fires, chemical reactions move ions across the synapse in channels. This changes the concentrations of the ions and in turn changes the electrical charge of the cells. Channels have gates on them that swing open and closed, as the action potential of the neuron is reached and then returned to the resting state.

NEURON

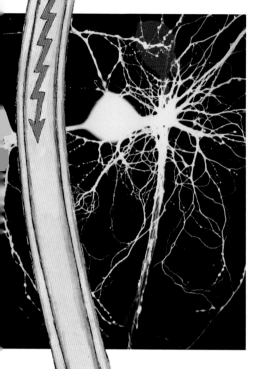

AXON

IMPULSES

NEUROTRANSMITTER

So we know we can change charge in a synapse by changing the kinds of ions there. This has to be very hard for the cell to do.

SODIUM
(NA+)

GATES

POTASSIUM
(K+)

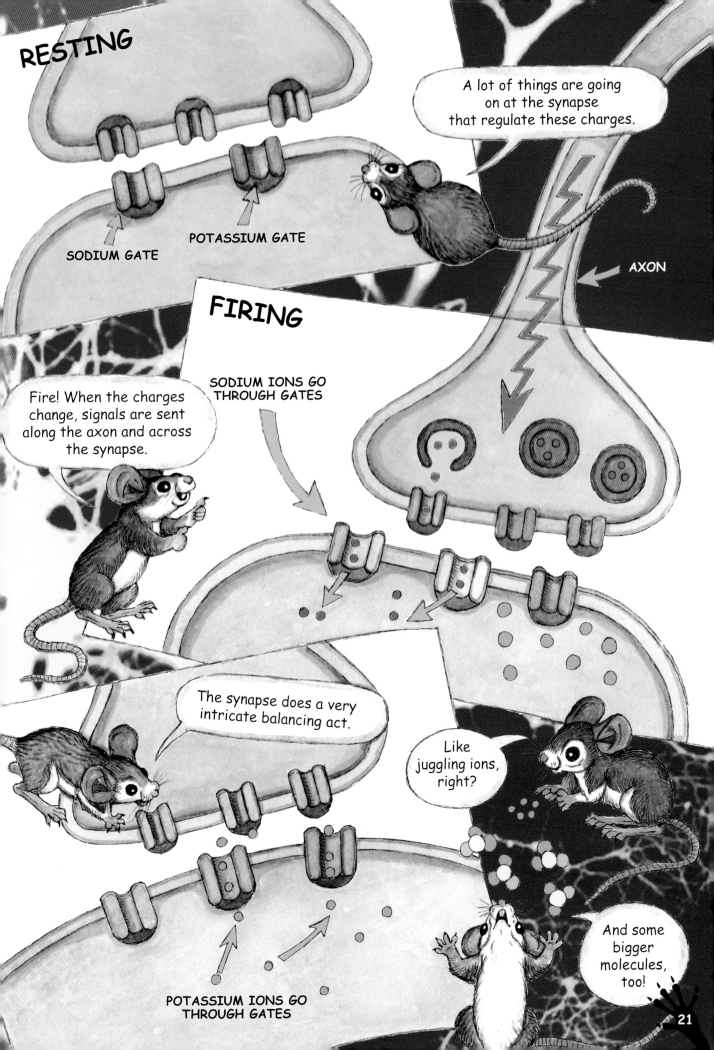

Neurotransmitters

Neurotransmitters do what their name suggests — they help the transmission of information between nerve cells. They can also slow down the transmission of information. Neurotransmitters can be small molecules or large molecules. An example of a small neurotransmitter is glutamate. It is perhaps the most important one of all. Glutamate tends to excite neural connections. An example of a larger neurotransmitter is dopamine, which tends

Okay. Patterns of connections and impulses make the brain work.

There are also molecules that affect the action potential firing across synapses.

Hmmm. And what kind of molecules are these?

FIRST CELL

NEUROTRANSMITTER MOLECULE

SYNAPSE

RECEPTOR

SECOND CELL

GLUTAMATE

to inhibit neural connections. Neurotransmitters are secreted from a nerve cell across a synapse to another nerve cell. They attach (bind) to receptors on the second cell. Depending on which receptors they bind to in the second cell, they either excite this second cell to spike an action potential or to inhibit it. And depending on whether they excite or inhibit action potentials molds the connections that are made in our brains by outside events.

Neurotransmitters. They come in all sizes and shapes. One of them is called dopamine.

NEUROTRANSMITTER MOLECULES

DOPAMINE

FIRST CELL

Just because I didn't know what a neurotransmitter is, is no reason to call me a name.

Sorry, Darwin but that's DOPE-A-MEEN.

SECOND CELL

So big deal, our brains make electricity. So can a potato!

But Darwin, it's the electricity and the chemicals making impulses that are stored in the cells of our brains which creates thought, memory, and other things.

Making it all work: Impulses

We can ask how does the light coming into your eyes get processed by your brain into the things you see. The light coming into the eye passes through the lens of your eye and then focuses on the retina. The retina is a very special tissue, a bunch of cells hooked up to the large optic nerve. Light hits the retina, and the cells there start to fire in specific response to different colors and shades of light. These retinal cells are attached to the optic nerve. The optic nerve carries impulses to a part of the brain called the lateral geniculate nucleus (or LGN for short). The electrical impulses are then transmitted all the way to the back of your brain by the optic nerve to the occipital lobe, where it is all processed.

RETINA

Wow! It's only a little electricity!!

LENS

It's how the electrical impulses are controlled that does the trick! It makes the way I think different from how you think!

So, you're claiming to have big impulses?

24

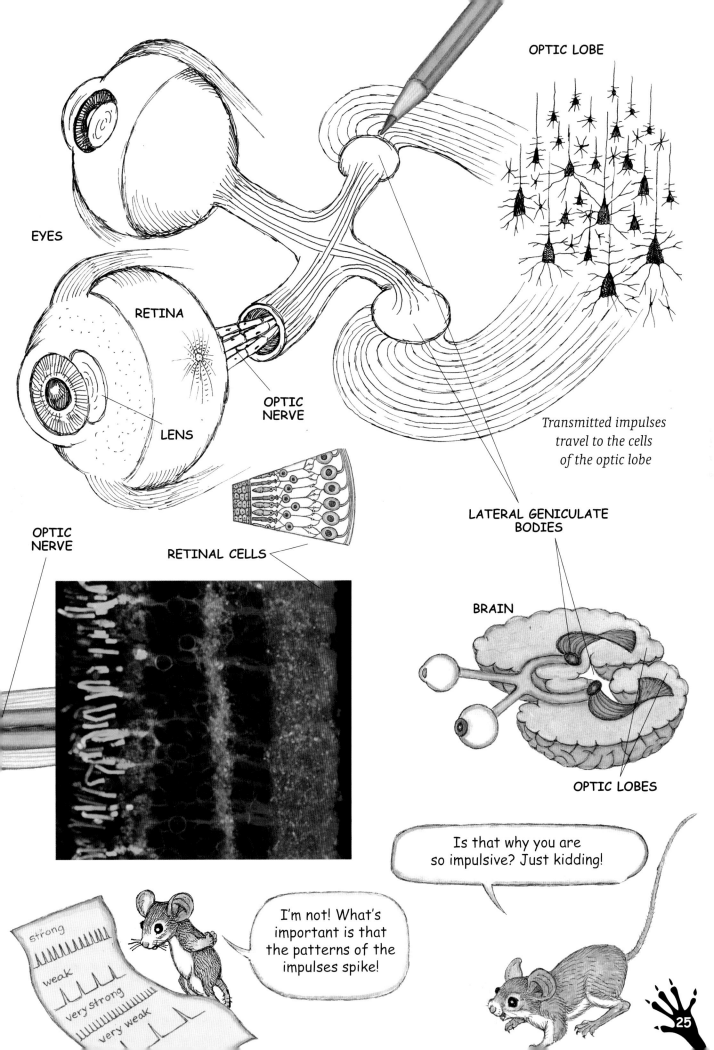

EYES

RETINA

LENS

OPTIC
NERVE

OPTIC
NERVE

RETINAL CELLS

OPTIC LOBE

*Transmitted impulses
travel to the cells
of the optic lobe*

LATERAL GENICULATE
BODIES

BRAIN

OPTIC LOBES

Is that why you are
so impulsive? Just kidding!

I'm not! What's
important is that
the patterns of the
impulses spike!

strong

weak

very strong

very weak

Connections

You are born with almost 100 billion neurons and a huge number of synapses. The nerve cells receive, interpret, store, and transmit information for your body. As you grow up, your nerve cells start to make connections with other neural cells in your brain. What you experience determines what neural connections are made. If you don't use certain neural cells or make connections, then they are lost — so use them, or lose them. The more experienced we become, the more neural connections we make, with each experience having a neural connection pathway associated with it. The good news is that these distinctive neural connections allow us to think fast when confronted with a particular situation. The bad news is that we are somewhat limited by these pathways. Instead of piecing together new patterns when we are confronted with new situations, our brains tend to follow the old, set-in-their-ways neural connections to process each new situation.

So . . . neurotransmitters and impulses explain how the things that happen all around us get into our brains.

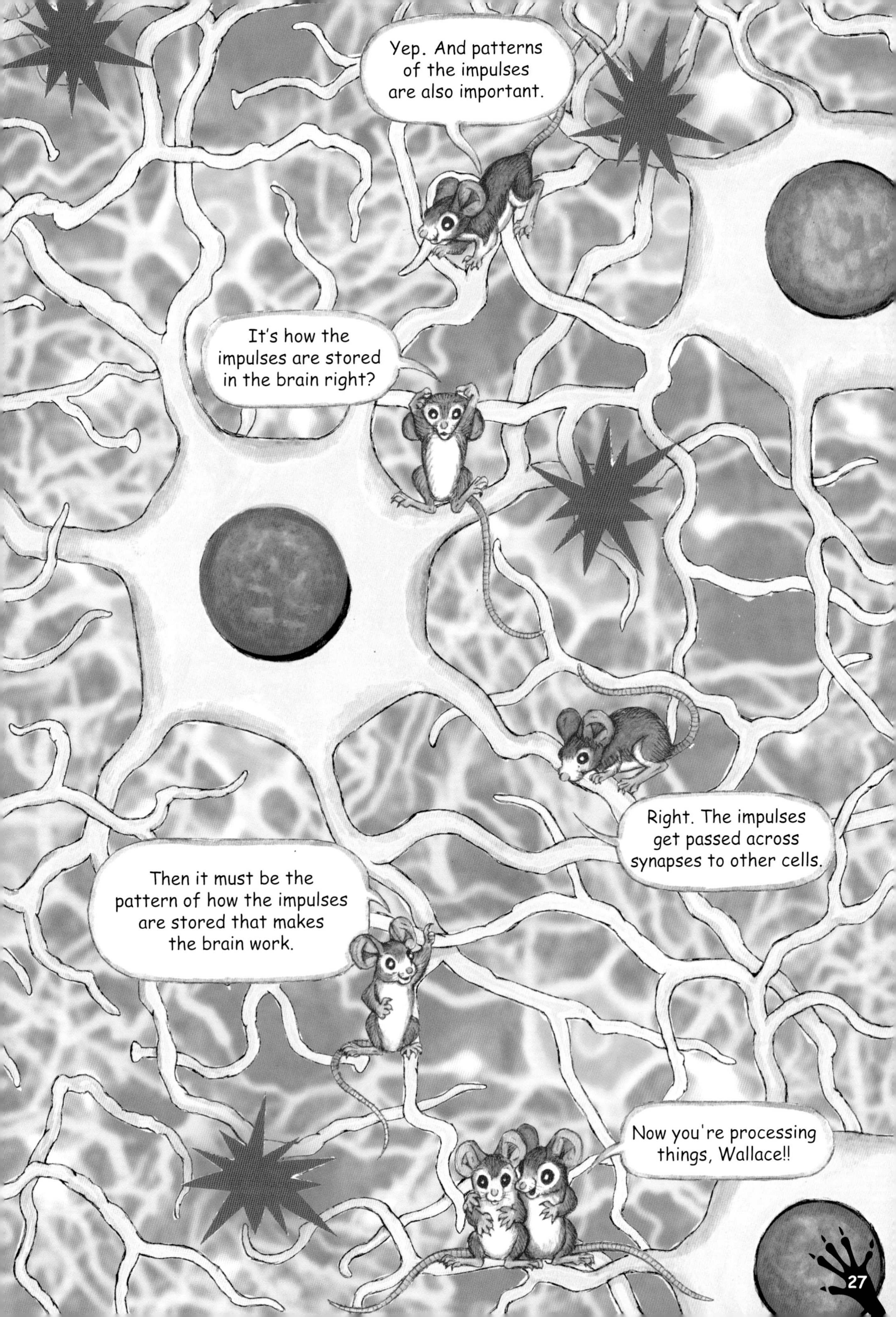

Yep. And patterns of the impulses are also important.
It's how the impulses are stored in the brain right?
Right. The impulses get passed across synapses to other cells.
Then it must be the pattern of how the impulses are stored that makes the brain work.
Now you're processing things, Wallace!!

HUMAN

CAT

Who are these weird creatures?

Your brain, spinal cord, and nerves make up your nervous system. Every second, the nervous system has to communicate huge amounts of information about the outside world to your brain. And your brain has to tell your body what to do through your nerves. The brain has two halves — right and left. Oddly enough, for most people the left half of the brain works for the right side of the body, and the right side of the brain works for the left side of the body.

HIP
TRUNK
SHOULDER
ELBOW HEAD
WRIST
LEG
FINGERS
FOOT
THUMB
TOES
EYE
NOSE
FACE
LIPS
TEETH
GUMS
JAW
TONGUE
THROAT

Dr. Wilder Penfield created these strange looking creatures you see here. He did this by touching various parts of the brains in people when they were having brain surgery, asking each patient what was felt. Penfield could do this because the brain doesn't feel pain. Amazingly, patients can have brain surgery while awake. Then Dr. Penfield drew the brains you see here, and marked where responses occurred when certain body parts were affected.

Our brains have two ways to move information around. One is called the motor system, and the other is called the sensory system. The motor system carries messages from the brain to different areas of the body that tell the body to move. The sensory system carries messages from the outside world through the nervous system to the brain, to tell the brain what is happening "outside." Each part of the body has cells involved in these systems.

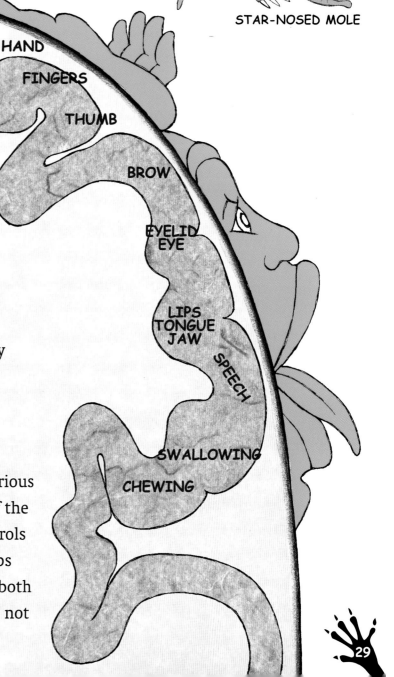

Talk about strange!

STAR-NOSED MOLE

HIP SHOULDER
KNEE ELBOW
ANKLE WRIST
HAND
FINGERS
THUMB
TOES
BROW
EYELID
EYE
LIPS
TONGUE
JAW
SPEECH
SWALLOWING
CHEWING

The creature on the left is called a sensory homunculus. It is a map of the sensory activity of a human brain. On the right is a motor homunculus. It maps the motor activity of the brain. All the creatures on these pages look so weird because the various parts of the body are drawn to the size of the corresponding area of the brain that controls the body part. For instance, while your lips have a huge area of the brain devoted to both sensory and motor activity, your hip does not have much devoted to either.

29

How do we look at brains?

The study of the brain is an old science. 100 years ago scientists who studied brains took advantage of accidents like Phineas Gage's, and also reports of strange illnesses. For instance, a scientist named Paul Broca heard about a person who suddenly could not speak using words in sentences. When this person died, Broca opened his skull and examined the brain, discovering a damaged area in one region of the brain. Broca suggested that this region controlled certain aspects of speaking. Another approach was used during brain surgery. Since some

Wait a minute. Scientists can't take brains out of our heads to look at them? Or can they?

Well, the first brain studies were made on people who were involved in accidents or had illnesses that altered their behavior, like Phineas Gage.

Phineas whoyamacallhim?

MOTOR PROGRAMING CENTER

MOTOR MOUTH REGION

WORD MEANING CENTER

BROCA'S AREA

WORD SOUNDING CENTER

Broca's area is the area of the brain where word meaning is processed.

Wilder Penfield created the homunculus. Penfield stimulated patients' brains during surgery, to determine which part of the brain controlled sensory and which part controlled motor function.

BRAIN CORTEX

patients can have brain surgery while awake, one can touch a part of the brain and ask the patient what happened. A Canadian surgeon named Wilder Penfield did this with several patients, and was able to map many interesting aspects of brain function.

GAGE! He was a rail worker who had an accident. A spike went straight through his head.

Ouch! That must have killed him?

WHERE THE SPIKE CAME OUT

SPIKE

WORD READING CENTER

VISUAL CORTEX

LIFE MASK

No, but it destroyed the small part of his brain that controls emotions and judgment The rest of his life, his behavior was drastically changed.

CEREBELLUM

PHINEAS GAGE

31

Looking at the brains of people in accidents must have been pretty slow going.

Must have been, but luckily scientists developed better ways to look at brains.

Like X-ray pictures, right?

How do scientists look at brains in the 21st century?

X-rays can look inside our bones and skin, but can take only take a two-dimensional image. The computed axial tomography (CAT) scan takes many pictures from a single reference point, and then uses a computer to put all the images together into a single picture or series of picture slices. The Magnetic Resonance Imaging (MRI) uses magnets to detect oxygen flow. Neuroscientists use a type of MRI called functional MRI (fMRI) which allows them to determine which part of a brain is used during specific thinking activities. When we use our brains for specific activities, oxygen flows more in those parts of the brain being used. So we can ask someone to sit in an MRI machine and remember something happy. What happens then is that the part of the brain that controls memories gets oxygen for working. The MRI then detects the flow of oxygen in the working part of the brain. Both the CAT scan and the MRI can take pictures of "slices" of the brain without really cutting the brain at all.

Right. X-rays were one of the first ways, but even better methods have been developed. Like the CAT scan.

CAT scan! I hate cats! I wouldn't want one of those for sure.

A person is placed in the machine and hundreds of pictures of the brain are taken. The process produces picture "slices" of the brain.

SLICES

And MRI was another.

Powerful computers are used to look at these pictures and give scientists an idea of what the brain looks like, without harming it.

That's magnetic resonance imaging.

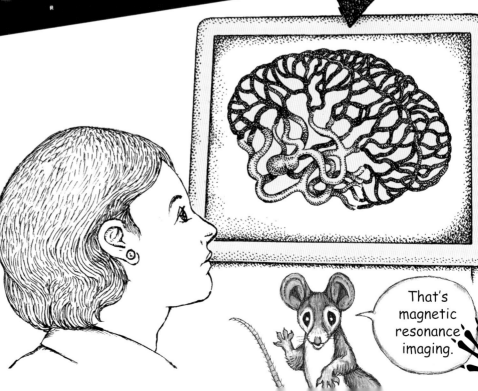

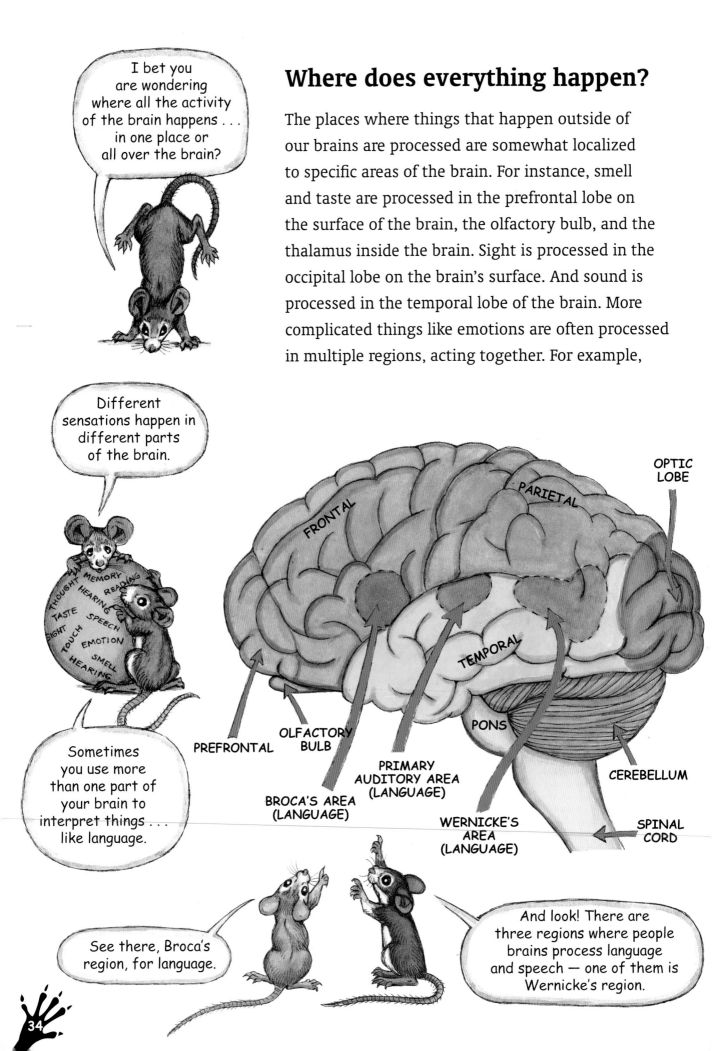

I bet you are wondering where all the activity of the brain happens . . . in one place or all over the brain?

Where does everything happen?

The places where things that happen outside of our brains are processed are somewhat localized to specific areas of the brain. For instance, smell and taste are processed in the prefrontal lobe on the surface of the brain, the olfactory bulb, and the thalamus inside the brain. Sight is processed in the occipital lobe on the brain's surface. And sound is processed in the temporal lobe of the brain. More complicated things like emotions are often processed in multiple regions, acting together. For example,

Different sensations happen in different parts of the brain.

THOUGHT MEMORY READING TASTE SPEECH SIGHT TOUCH EMOTION SMELL HEARING HEARING

Sometimes you use more than one part of your brain to interpret things . . . like language.

OPTIC LOBE

FRONTAL

PARIETAL

TEMPORAL

PREFRONTAL

OLFACTORY BULB

PRIMARY AUDITORY AREA (LANGUAGE)

BROCA'S AREA (LANGUAGE)

PONS

WERNICKE'S AREA (LANGUAGE)

CEREBELLUM

SPINAL CORD

See there, Broca's region, for language.

And look! There are three regions where people brains process language and speech — one of them is Wernicke's region.

memory is processed in the occipital, parietal, and frontal lobes on the surface of the brain, and the hippocampus and inner cerebellum inside the brain. But some really important functions — like emotions — are processed in very specific areas of the brain. Emotions, for instance, are processed by the amygdala. Tools like fMRI will help to map these regions even better.

Over the years, neuroanatomists have mapped the brain both inside and out. The maps are very important for determining the functions of the brain.

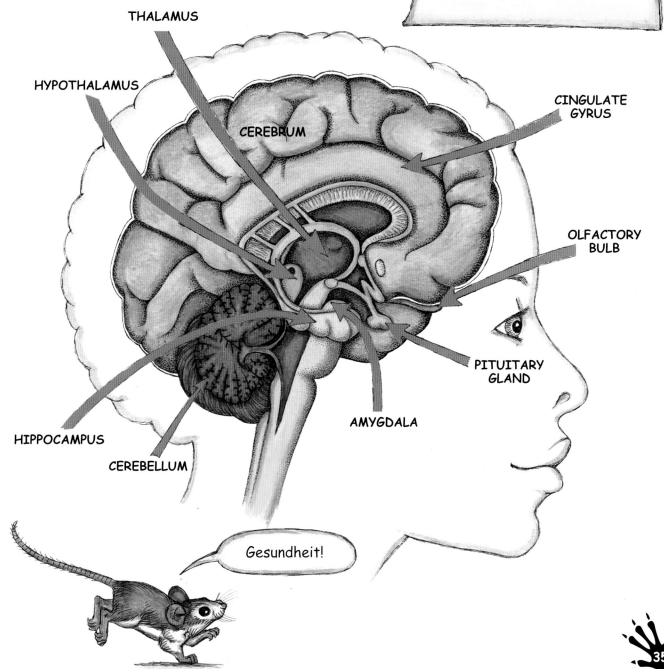

THALAMUS

HYPOTHALAMUS

CEREBRUM

CINGULATE GYRUS

OLFACTORY BULB

PITUITARY GLAND

AMYGDALA

HIPPOCAMPUS

CEREBELLUM

Gesundheit!

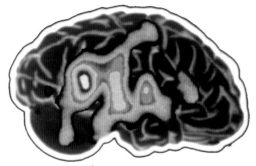

This brain shows the human brain hearing.

Your Senses and Your Brain

How your senses work determines how you perceive the outside world. In these two pictures of the brain we see positron emission tomography (PET) scans of human brains.

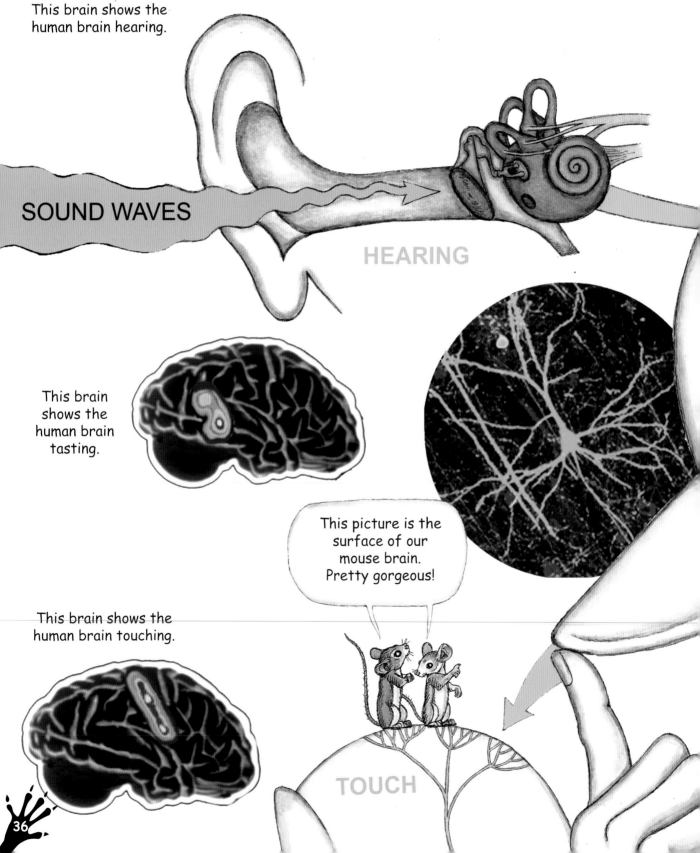

SOUND WAVES

HEARING

This brain shows the human brain tasting.

This picture is the surface of our mouse brain. Pretty gorgeous!

This brain shows the human brain touching.

TOUCH

In these scans, areas of the brain that are active during a specific task are colored red and yellow, any region with a lot of yellow and red is working hard during the specific task.

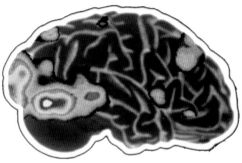

This brain shows the human brain seeing.

By doing these kinds of experiments, a "map" of the brain like this one can be generated.

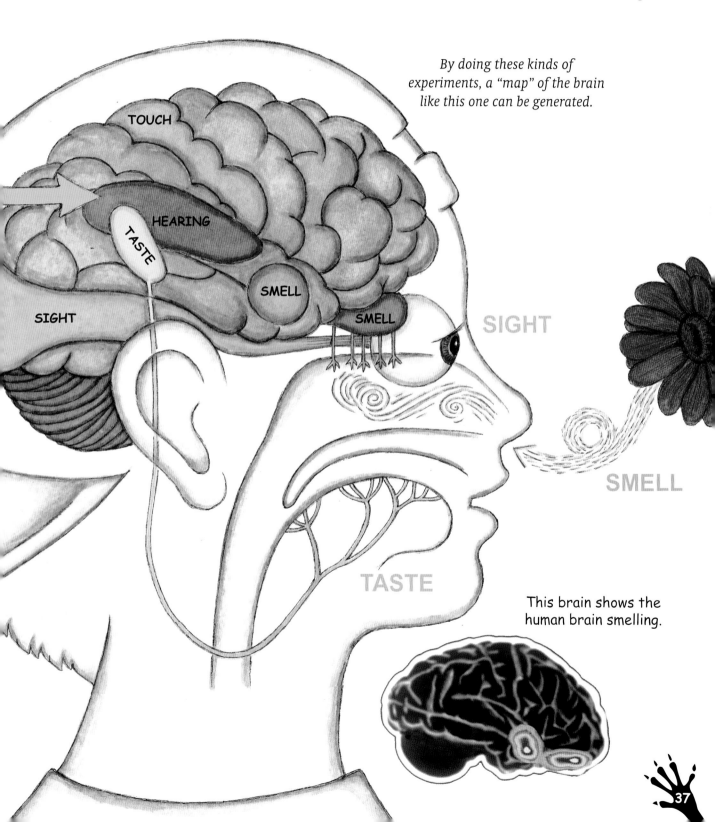

TOUCH

HEARING

TASTE

SMELL

SMELL

SIGHT

SIGHT

SMELL

TASTE

This brain shows the human brain smelling.

Different kinds of memory

Our current understanding of memory comes from putting together information from psychologists who study the behavior of memory, and from neuroscientists who study the chemistry and physiology of memory. Memory is often described by the kinds of memories we have — like implicit and explicit, or short-term and long-term. For instance, implicit memories are those that we recognize with our conscious mind, and know we remember these things — like remembering where we put the sunflower seeds. Explicit memories, on the other hand, are things our brains remember, but are more basic to our survival — like remembering to pull

And there are other memories that keep us from doing stupid things without even thinking.

Like not sticking your paw in the fire?

I'm just trying to remember where I put those sunflower seeds this morning, for my snack.

our hand away from something hot. Even more complex things — like bike riding — eventually become explicit memories. Explicit memories are those that are used when we say "Oh, I could do that in my sleep." Scientists have found that nerve cells involved in explicit memory can alter their shape and the amount of neurotransmitters they produce. Specifically, explicit memory is caused by the holding back of neurotransmitters at synapses, as well as changes in the cell shape and connections in the brain. Explicit memory actually results in physical changes of both chemistry and nerve cell structure in your brain. Your brain actually gets wired differently for different kinds of memories.

That's implicit memory!

4250

The American Museum of Natural
No. 200715 . Date 24 April
Panthera leo.
No. data ....
Dr. Tower .... #59.
Eyes in Alc

mesoplodon jaw oil

Our brains fill in things when we see incomplete or partial images. For instance, while the triangle that points up looks like it has lines in it. It really doesn't. This is because your brain is filling in what it doesn't see.

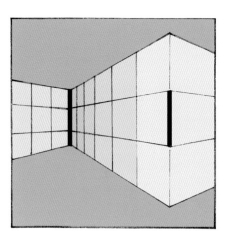

Perception!

How we perceive different things that are around us is a matter of our brains interpreting the impulses. But impulses have a number of ways of being interpreted. Scientists suggest that there are two basic ways to explain this — "top-down" and "bottom-up." In "top-down" processing, the brain gets the impulses, detects the pattern of the impulses, and then rapidly tries to combine the patterns into more recognizable patterns. Finally, the brain takes the recognizable pattern and interprets it. The other way the brain could process information is what is called "bottom-up" processing. This process takes the impulses and makes a guess at what the impulses mean. The brain then rapidly attempts to assess the impulses to see if the guess is right or wrong. Once the brain has tested enough guesses, it then interprets what the impulses mean. Both top-down and bottom-up processing happen very, very fast.

Which black line is longer?

But the brain can interpret things in a lot of different ways. It's the way your nerve cells are connected and your past experiences that help you interpret the impulses.

Sure. The impulses from our eyes detect different colors, shapes, and sizes that our brain processes.

What do you see, faces or vases?

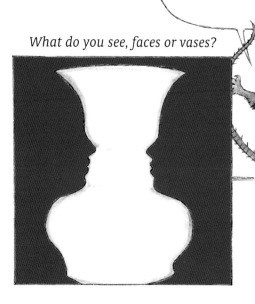

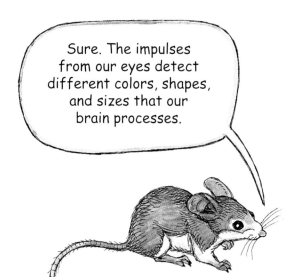

I wonder what happens to my brain when I sleep.

I know. We do something interesting with our eyes. Ever watch a cat sleep?

What is sleep?

We know that when we are awake, our brains are transmitting a lot of electrical impulses. The very active alpha and beta waves our brains make, are the product of this awake brain activity. When we sleep, our brain activity changes and we make delta and theta waves instead. Why do we sleep? Scientists think that we sleep because we need downtime to allow our brains to process the events of the previous day. Our brains need time to incorporate what we have seen, felt, smelt, heard, and tasted, with all of our previous knowledge and memories. The best way to do this is to sleep. During sleep, we also engage in an interesting physical activity involving our eyes. Underneath our eyelids, our eyes

Are you kidding? I hate cats!

Well, if you *did* watch a cat sleep, you would notice that their eyes move under their eyelids. It's called rapid eye movement (REM).

twitch and move a lot during some periods of sleep. These periods are called rapid eye movement (REM) sleep. Periods of sleep when we don't experience REM are called non-REM (NREM). We need both REM and NREM sleep to accomplish a good night's sleep, and to adequately incorporate the previous day's information. We spend about 25 percent of our sleep time in REM, and the remainder in NREM.

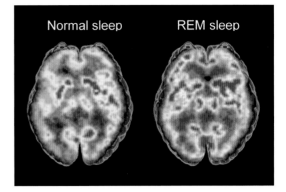

Normal sleep   REM sleep

Positron emission tomography (PET) is another kind of brain imaging. It also shows the activity of brains during specific tasks. The brain on the left shows a person sleeping without rapid eye movements. The brain on the right shows a person having REM during sleep.

Stage One	Stage Two	Stage Three	Stage Four	Stage Five
light sleep / muscle twitching	breathing and heart rate show slight decrease in body temperature	deep sleep begins / delta waves begin	very deep sleep / rythmic breathing / delta waves	rapid eye movement (REM) / dreaming / breathing and heart rate speed up

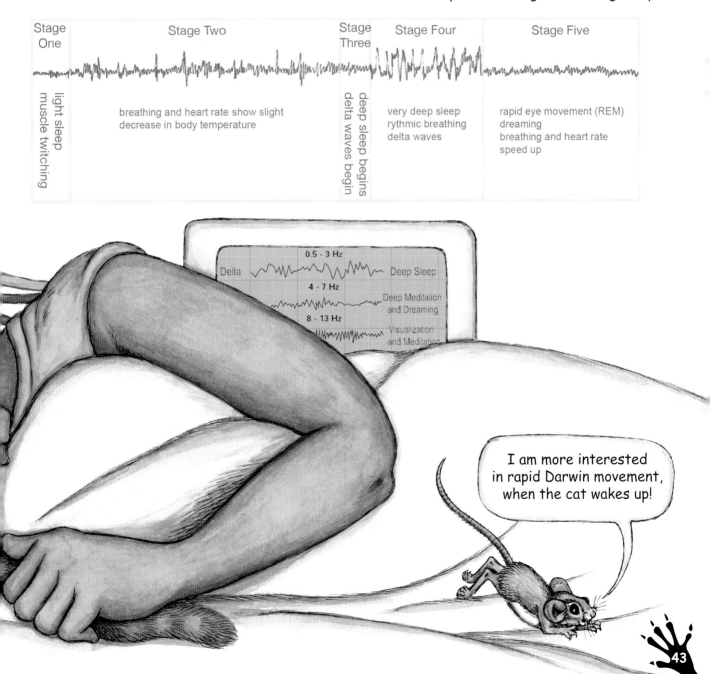

0.5 - 3 Hz
Delta   Deep Sleep
4 - 7 Hz
               Deep Meditation and Dreaming
8 - 13 Hz
               Visualization and Meditation

I am more interested in rapid Darwin movement, when the cat wakes up!

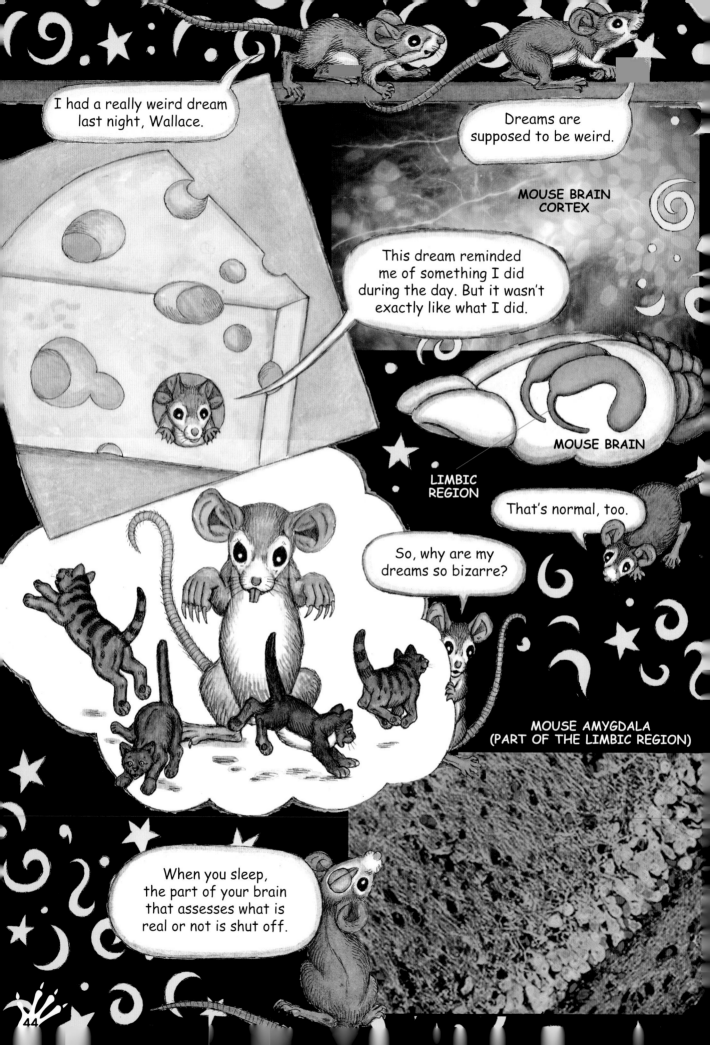

What is a dream?

When you sleep, certain areas of your brain remain active and others shut down. For instance, a part of your brain, the limbic region, remains active. This brain area is in almost all animals, so it is considered ancient. The limbic region controls emotions like fear that were important to early animals' survival. On the other hand, another part of your brain — the dorsal lateral pre-frontal cortex — is shut down during dreaming. Decisions and assessing reality (rationality) are the jobs of this part of the brain. But this region of the brain isn't the only area responsible for assessing reality, and the other areas that do this work aren't shut off when we sleep, so there are still parts of the brain checking reality during dreams. Put all of this together, and it explains a lot about dreams. Since the rational center of our brains is shut off during dreaming, we have weird images in our dreams, but not too weird. We also tend to have very emotional dreams, because the emotional part of our brain remains stimulated. Because the part of our brains controlling memory remains on, we can bring memories into our dreams.

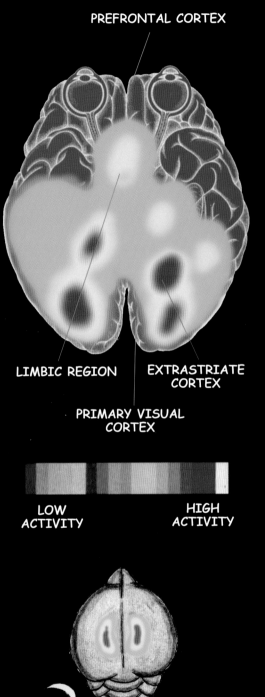

DREAMING HUMAN BRAIN
SEEN FROM THE TOP

PREFRONTAL CORTEX

LIMBIC REGION

EXTRASTRIATE CORTEX

PRIMARY VISUAL CORTEX

LOW ACTIVITY

HIGH ACTIVITY

You mean I can't decide what is real and what isn't? No wonder my dreams are so weird.

Remember, animals like flies and worms and other things have really small brains. This doesn't mean that they can't do brainy things. Watch this sea snail.

It's an Aplysia. Just like worms and flies, it can actually remember things!

Do animals like flies and snails remember things?

How nerve cells work at the chemical level is one of the most important questions in all of biology. Scientists can use animals like snails and flies and worms to study how nerve cells work. Because they can be easily bred and trained in the lab, these organisms are great to study. One of the neatest experiments done in all of science involves using a very ugly looking sea snail called Aplysia to unravel how nerve cells work. A scientist named Dr. Eric Kandel used this animal to understand memory. He would slightly shock the siphon of this sea snail, and this would cause the gills of the animal to jump back. He would then study the changes in molecules in cells after the shock. Dr. Kandel won a Nobel Prize for his work on Aplysia, proving that even the ugliest and simplest of animals can actually be beautiful.

GANGLION

A ganglion is another name for a complex of nerves.

I beg your pardon! Who are you calling ugly!

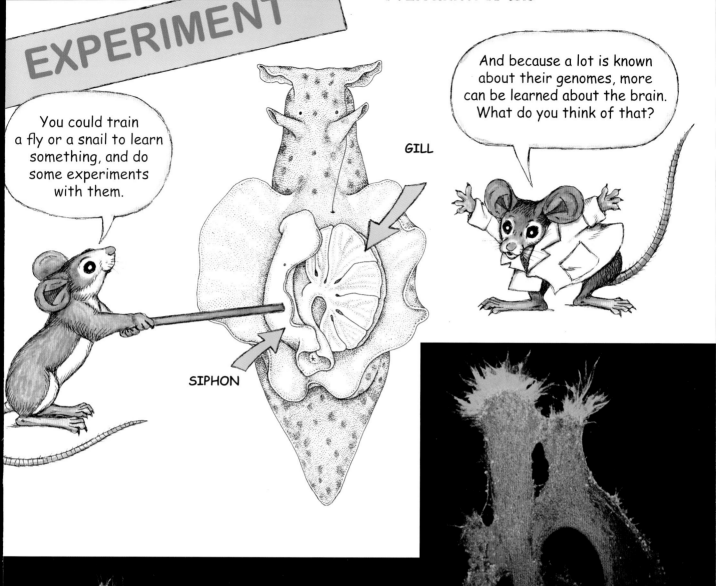

You could train a fly or a snail to learn something, and do some experiments with them.

And because a lot is known about their genomes, more can be learned about the brain. What do you think of that?

GILL

SIPHON

While this photo looks a lot like the snail's antenna, it is really a microscope picture of nerves. So don't get confused.

Look at these beautiful Aplysia nerves!

Wallace, I hate to tell you this, but we don't really have regions in our brains for speech or language.

I kinda guessed that. I figured we needed a little more brain power for that.

Consciousness — or the ability to think about thinking — is a uniquely human characteristic. Sorry.

Well, knock me over with a feather. I guess that means I don't have a sense of myself?

Squeak!
Squeak!
Squeak!
Squeak!
Squeak!
Sque
Squeak!
Squeak!

Thinking about thinking

Humans are the only organisms on the planet that can think about thinking. We are unique in this respect, because of the way our brains evolved. The way our brains evolved has influenced the unique way our brains are organized. It is the organization of the human brain that makes us able to do the things we do. We are the only species on the planet that can think about our past and future, and place them into the context of our present. Does this mean we are better than other organisms on the planet? Most certainly not! It just means that we are different from other life on the planet.

Don't worry. We'll be back!

www.bunkerhillpublishing.com
First published in 2010
by Bunker Hill Publishing Inc.
285 River Road, Piermont, New Hampshire 03779, USA

10 9 8 7 6 5 4 3 2 1

Text copyright © Rob DeSalle and Patricia J. Wynne
Artwork copyright © Patricia J. Wynne
Photographs and Illustrations copyright American
    Museum of Natural History
Photo credits: AMNH (pages 2, 3, 8); Van Wedeen (cover,
    page 6); William Kristan (page 12); Elain Bearer
    (page 18); Micha Spira (pages 20, 21, 46, 47); Andreas
    Reichenbach (page 25)

Library of Congress Control Number: 2010931629
ISBN 9781593730857

Published in the United States by Bunker Hill Publishing
Designed by Peter Holm, Sterling Hill Productions
Printed in China by Jade Productions

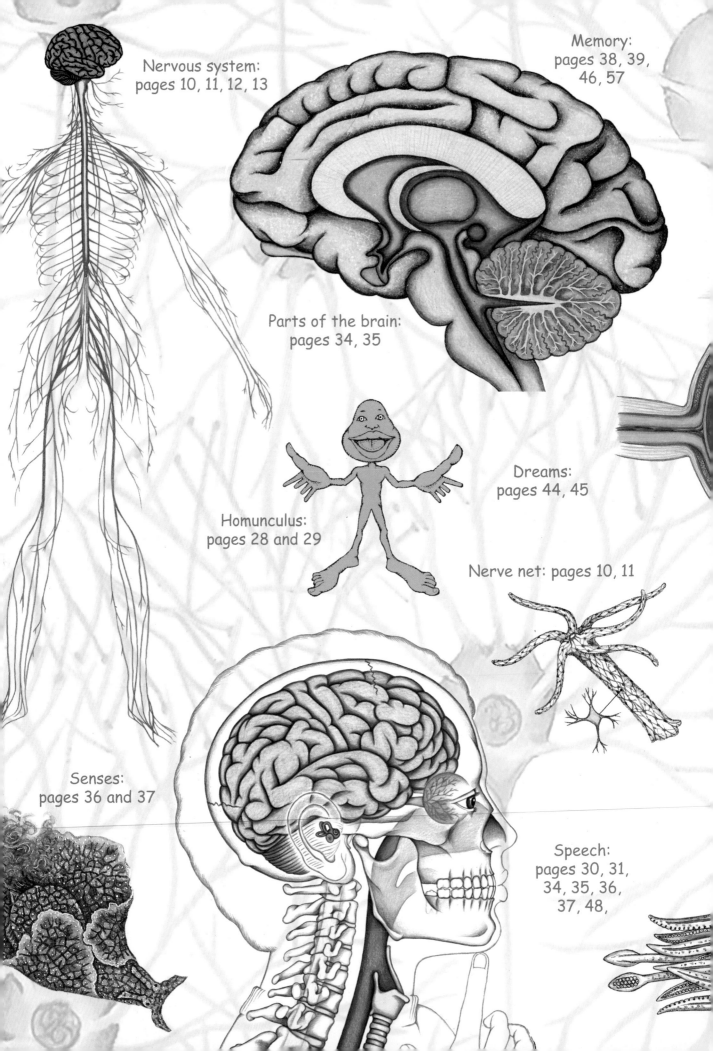